Heroes, Advise Us

Heroes, advise us

Poems by ADRIEN STOUTENBURG

CHARLES SCRIBNER'S SONS, NEW YORK

3/1981
Genl

For Laura

CONTENTS

Heroes, Advise Us

ONE
This Journey

THIS JOURNEY

> To the memory of Captain Robert F. Scott
> and his four companions, Dr. E. A. Wilson,
> Lieutenant H. R. Bowers, Captain L. E. Oates,
> and Edgar Evans, seaman, who reached the
> South Pole, January 1912, only to find that
> they had been preceded by Roald Amundsen.
> All five perished on the return journey.

I

THE LAND

That world was some glass-maker's error,
a heap of tumblers pouring wind
and the stems of mountains breaking,
panes and blown patterns grinding
into the whale-backed sea
where clouds froze to drowning statues.
Furnace or hand went cold;
the dying bellows wheezed
with a reptile sigh
and the epoch became a diamond
larger than us and Australia coupled,
yet left one peak steaming like a horse
over the still and fruitless meadows.

The continent creaks on its wide gallows,
perpetual skull with a blizzard's hair
and the weedless eyes of lost explorers
staring at petrels blown like more snow
in the wind's cape. Skua gulls, web-footed,
make a trail of red leaves
around the penguin's blinded child.
Hot food is sweet, as dead men know

who crawled through the skull,
drank bloodless tea,
kicked back the killer
at the world's wild edge,
dragged their shadows like fallen beggars
until the blue spice of a crevasse
whipped their nostrils and they saw the land open
down trenches of jackknives;
hung in harness, pulled their shadows closer,
staggered on to the deeper crystal,
found the killer, at the center, waiting.

All maps are drawn where men have drawn
their own hearts over the unknown landscape,
and the cloven brain imagines ravines
more easily crossed than its own fissures.
There a man walked on common water.
Here five sank through the transparent world
into a death we sometimes remember.

The last expedition is never the last
and loaves of frost are never divided
into a multitude of fishes,
and the skua must feed on the kidney he finds
or the eyes that come like a light to meet him
in his hunger-darkness. The hooked beak drives
all but speech into the waste
of breaking tumblers and grinding patterns,
and words are written.

THE WORDS (From Scott's Journal)

The small green tent and the great white road . . .
The hiss of the primus . . .
The whine of a dog . . .
The neigh of our steeds . . .

The driving cloud of powdered snow . . .
    Two minutes in the open makes a white figure . . .
The crunch of footsteps . . .
The eternal silence . . .
The blizzard . . .
The crevasses . . .

The deep, dreamless sleep that follows . . .

SCOTT

He was strenuous, neat,
almost too proper,
cried like a woman,
grew faint at blood,
polished his medals,
made service a savior,
stood for his portrait
with his thinning hair parted,
worshipped the Navy,
adored his mother,
loved his wife,
wanted his son
to study nature;
shot his bolt, muddled,
missed getting through,
proved that the English
can die well on their journeys;

walked nine hundred miles out
and a million miles back,
wrote fevered letters
with an icy pencil,
consoling widows, brothers, fathers,
scrawled, "My whole heart
goes out in pity,"

studied his blackening toes
and wondered
if the knife would hurt
if it came to cutting;

remembered Evans,
the giant treasure;
remembered Oates,
tender with ponies,
both of them under
the great road and whitening;
studied the silver sloth of his hand
unable to make a pencil stamp
as feet had stamped,
stumbled, pounded
to batter the miles
like bloody hammers
to the last tent,
   the last word,
      the beginning of mercy.

       He was too thorough,
         Strung action out
       Beyond the dream's limit,
         Packed his doubt

       On a sticking sledge.
         His own ghost straddled
       The runner's edge
         And the wind raddled

       Hope and despair
         Into one white braid;
       He was never a coward
         But half-afraid

To be less than a hero;
   Had put behind him
The weakling's itch
   To sit by the dim

Hot light of books
   And a country fire.
Duty demanded
   That purpose acquire

Muscles and dogs.
   He made the endeavor,
Took one step,
   And went on forever.

II

THE JOURNEY OUT

They left their base and October behind them,
the flag of empire curled on their sledges,
lured by the world's end, the southern tiptoe,
hub where all spokes of the turning map
plunged to a dot they could be first to conquer:
twelve men, eight ponies, the Russian dogs
running and tumbling, the ponies' manes lifting
like little trees. Horses hated the wind,
foraged for shelter, bucked at the death-smell
from a far glacier where they would be freed
of loads forever, their bullet-smoked haunches
sorted and eaten; ribs, hearts, liver
stored in a cairn flying the black flag
of a darker nation.

Oates

Oates, the dragoon, the Iniskillin lover
of horseflesh and crystal and argent adventure,
tobacco-chewer, slogger, judge of stallions,
wrestled cold manes, fussed with fodder,
oil cakes, bran, built barns out of blizzards,
coaxed the pale hoofs of conquest closer,
heard the mare's whinny on the wind,
stroked a muzzle with pity in his palm,
said their names over and tried to forget them—
Jehu and Nobby, Chinaman, Snatcher—
chewed his pity and coughed it out
to make a brown flower in a white stable.

Tractors led the way, mechanical hope
riding on rollers, engines shuddering
in the hot cold that fired blizzards
into white sparks. Marchers, trapped
on blowing pavements, cheered the machines
they had not believed in, and their leader
hoped in spite of not hoping
while his great toys groaned across the Barrier
and the white road was blotched
with their black drippings
for a day, two days, five days, seven . . .

The throttle froze to the engineer's fingers
and his breath stroked like another engine,
knowing the metal veins could burst
and the rollers break like the ice
on his forehead, but driving, driving
into the waste.
                      Cylinders split
in the crush of cold and the dark snouts rolled
into their graves without a whinny,

black ribs, black spines, dead spark and throttle
left to the jaws of a thousand winters.

Tracks of ponies, dogs, man-haulers
made a blue wreath of footsteps around them,
going on toward the Beardmore ice and the summit
and the bullets waiting for Chinaman and Jehu.
All could not last until the glacier
and these were the crocks, the weakening members.

 Jehu went first,
 made four feedings
 for the dogs which must run
 their longer journey.

 Chinaman walked
 to the brink of December.

 The rest limped on
 with their manes blowing,
 only four bags
 of fodder among them
 and seventy miles
 to the end of their haul—
 hundreds more for men—
 and the land showing peaks
 through the window of distance.
 The window broke
 and the tents trembled
 like the green skin
 of pointed beasts,
 while only time marched
 toward any conquest.

 Four days and four nights
 and ribs showing.

One must stick it out
and hope for the best.
In a brief spell of hope
last night
one heard laughter.

But rations must be stolen
from the future
for the howl of wind
was the howl of hunger
in spite of red, sweet
bones and haunches—
Christopher, Michael—
food for dogs
and English heroes.

It is evil to lie here . . .
watching the mottled
wet green walls of our tent,
the glistening wet bamboos,
the bedraggled sopping socks . . .
to hear the falling snow
and the ceaseless rattle
of fluttering canvas . . .
to feel the wet clinging dampness
of everything touched.
Add the stress of sighted failure
of our whole plan . . .
But, yet, after all,
one can go on striving . . .

Wilson

Sleeping bags were wet, but Wilson drew
the dry profile of a penguin in his diary,
the lean hand dreaming of rookeries
he had not reached through a hell of trying;

doctor, scholar, "tough as steel in the traces,"
although he had lived through thirty-nine winters
(but no summer like this)
with a spirit designed to burn through drifts
or hack a cliff down for the sake of a glint
of an unknown mica, metal, fossil.
Birds' eggs had beauty, and the aurora
streaming like the hair of a tall mermaid.
He sketched them, carried their brittle portraits
among the flags and food, and the opium
saved for some moment of decision,
while his pockets creaked
with stone discoveries.
One could never be weighed down
by the granite of knowledge,
and snow-blind eyes could see the glory
of conquest and science standing together
where he and Scotty would stand and unfold
the Union Jack on the turning axis.

They marched again,
the last march for ponies.
One pony endured
on a feast of biscuits
a lean hand spared
from its gaunt, day's ration.

Men, said the doctor
to his windy stomach,
could endure hunger
better than horses,
and watched Nobby canter
on stilts like legs—
and dreaded the bullet
that life required.

Bowers

At the beginning he was never cold,
wore his earlaps up, sweated in storms,
burned a wick that kept him going
like a furious elf swatting the knees
of something intolerable in the way.
"Birdie," they called when a thing needed seeing
or just seeing through. His eyes were small;
his nose would have hampered a larger man,
but he focused over a thousand miles
to the cold prize, saw the giant overthrown
and huddled beneath his straddling thighs.

He was the youngest of the five,
lieutenant, marine, captain of stores,
guardian of chocolate, pemmican, tea
and caches left for gnawing hands;
helper, hauler, contemptuous of sleep,
builder of trees out of paper and sticks
for Christmas in June—the branches gleamed
above a castle of foolish gifts,
whistles and popguns; handler of silk
where weather balloons like the wobbling heads
of strange, drowsy children
nodded against the birdless wind;
photographer, too, who found his lens
turned on a wizened, withering thing,
the Norwegian's banner clapping behind.
He trudged on legs as short as thumbs,
though lengthening to match his eyes,
and traveled farther than he knew.

> *The wind rises and falls . . .*
> *We are struggling on,*
> *considering all things,*
> *against the odds.*

Ponies were dead, the dogs sent back.
　He led his eleven up a road
　Of buried glass where the glacier flowed
Like an old man's beard, mourned the lack

Of reasonable weather, and envied such ice
　As Shackleton found, blue under foot,
　Silk for sledges; scribbled a note
To those in the vise

Of a rear-guard camp, "I never felt fitter,"
　Took time to brag, "I keep up with the rest."
　But things were not rosy. The test
Remained and the going was bitter.

He did his sums, measured his men,
　Subtracted three for the last run,
　Saw Bowers' eyes and added one
In spite of the plan, went on again,

Shaping farewell to the other seven—
　Good fellows all, but all could not go.
　Through green goggles he watched the snow
Fall like a city, and fought for vision.

Evans

This was the strong man, fixer of sledges,
six feet tall, two-hundred pound mast
for hope to lean on. A royal seaman,
he learned to ride an unruled ocean
beyond one empire to another, but found
strength could plunge like a falling anchor
through the steep foam of shoreless blizzards.
His brain was a cupboard hoarding details
of crampons, ski shoes, each thread and tool

that made the machinery of triumph
more supple; corrected faults of harness
and will but could not mend a deepening fault
that traveled with him, felt himself dwindle,
supporting a giant whose open mouth,
crammed with wind, swallowed whole dreams
of beef and mutton.
                              Rations were equal
for equal courage. Honor demanded
the hoosh be measured, biscuits divided
between lean and stalwart. He asked nothing more,
but his long bones ranted, clattered like teeth,
down the thinning miles.

I

Huge, uninhabited, roughly circular,
highest of the continents, windiest, coldest,
hardest to reach, perpetually hostile,
pivot where the polar anticyclone snarls
seaward from the sepulchres of upheaved mountains.

In five million square miles no walking beast
leaves the blue stamp of paw or hoof,
and only wind, or the southern lights
singing like rayon, charges the silence.
Voices are unknown except for those of pilgrims
climbing the bleak, ascending forehead
of a plateau that ends in constellations
where the true cross shines like a golden raft,
guide of mariners on a midnight ocean.
Larger and lower, the false crucifix
lures the unwary, and betrays.

Only the rootless snow makes meadows,
yet glaciers hold in their gray coffins

dead spines of fern, the fossil lace
of sequoia leaves, while Mount Erebus,
large as a nation,
blows fire from his spuming lip
like sparks of nameless, falling birds.

Some tropic memory haunts the wind
and neither men nor mountains know
what root is straining underfoot,
what branches are reaching overhead.

I had pinned my faith
on better conditions . . .
We can but toil on . . .

far from England,
snow melting into walls
around their knees,
crossbars trapped
in the sweating drifts,
two-hundred pound sledges
moving, barely,
reaching two thousand feet
and fog,
and sly crevasses,
blue lips in the beard.
Men went down to the length of a harness,
like breaking through a glass house . . .
As first man, I get first chance.
It's exciting not knowing
which step will give way.

Camp forty-six, altitude eight thousand.
The wind is continuous from the south-southeast,
      very searching . . .
and about us is a scene of the wildest desolation,
but we are a very cheerful party
and tomorrow is Christmas Day . . .

Night camp fifty-one, height nine thousand.
There have been some hours of very steady plodding . . .
these are the best part of the business,
they mean forgetfulness and advance.

Night camp fifty-four. Fourteen below.
A stick of chocolate to celebrate the New Year.

Camp fifty-six. The summit of farewell
for the five going on and the returning party,
only one hundred and forty-six miles
between them now and the white magnet.

The captain hated his role, dreaded the hurt
of those not chosen for the last hazard.
One man wept. The others pulled masks
over their faces, shook hands and turned,
and one remembered for forty years after
the diminishing specks, five dots on a scroll
of illimitable gray, the tall wind behind,
and the horizon curling upward and over.

Camp fifty-eight. Twenty-three below.
We sigh for a breeze to sweep the hard snow.
We go little over a mile and a quarter an hour now . . .
it is a big strain as the shadows creep slowly round
from our right through ahead to our left.
What lots of things we think of . . .
What castles one builds now hopefully that the Pole is ours.

Under the ice was a deeper danger
   his mind skidded on. He pulled fear tight,
braced it with pride. He was no sprinter.
   Science was the rock. But still the white,
loping sun held the shadow
   of that other figure which had started before him.
Nights in a night-assaulted tent
   he found his dreams stapled to the rim
of a yapping void, saw Amundsen's dogs
   with flapping tongues gallop past
his lame ponies, woke with sweat
   caught in his hands, glimpsed a vast
landscape of teeth on end, turned to his letters,
   trusting in language to deliver a meaning
beyond disaster. *It's the work that counts,*
   not the applause that follows. The wild, leaning
canvas became a sky flung across cricket fields and
      ships.
   Racing was not what one went out for,
but hope reared on legs as hard as the whips
   rapped over a shuddering spine of huskies
his dread sent toward the revolving shrine
   hung between antipodal seas, the blended oceans,
         and the hard whine
         of continuing silence,
         continuing marches—
         camp sixty-one,
         sixty-two,
         sixty-five,
and the killer at the center, waiting.

> *All is new ahead . . .*
> *Our chance still holds . . .*
> *We have covered six miles*
> *but at fearful cost . . .*

Another hard grind
and five miles added . . .
All the time the sledge
rasps and creaks.
We ought to get through . . .
but, oh! for a better surface . . .
So close it seems
and only the weather to baulk us.

Only the weather and fatigue and hunger
and the cold cutting deeper in spite of sunlight.
Oates, slogging on through whinnying silence,
fancied at times he heard the brittle
step of a pony just behind him
and felt a red ghost nuzzle his shoulder.
Evans chewed the wind, tried not to remember
the taste of things glowing in ovens
or sprouting green out of a garden.
The sky was warmer, the drifts softened,
but cold had become an interior host
dressed and marching in their bodies.
Even Bowers, the "little marvel," felt the chill
drive through some invisible doorway
to reach the fire under his ribs
though the fire in his legs still blazed,
while Wilson, leaning against the traces,
considered the medicines in his bag
and found no antidote but marching
another mile, three miles, four,
heard Scott breathing hard beside him.
The breath seemed his own. He had written,
"There is nothing I would not do for him,"
rewrote it now on the smoking air,
stumbled, straightened, made another mile,
grateful to be there, glad to be chosen.

This is the land of superior mirages,
distortions, dreams, repeated rainbows,
false sunsets and deceptive sunrises,
ships overturned yet serenely riding
the high abyss as if to some anchor
hung between Polaris and the Goat.

The wisest visitors have been misled,
followed the wrong image, found themselves
trapped in a hall of carnival mirrors
where the glassy air's inverted lens
reflects an insupportable landscape,
makes grotesque the simplest being,
and holds the golden oasis forever
one inch away from the scheming hand.

Even at the gate where the first floes drift
like dead messengers from some wrinkled tomb,
the *fata morgana* magnifies and lifts
the wind's debris into steeples,
hoists cathedrals against the sky,
erects such cities, a pilgrim imagines
Atlantis risen with all its green towers,
garlands, and women, and stalks through the crystal
into the darkness behind every mirror.

Early explorers followed a mirage
twisting with angels and horny fires,
recorded phantoms as veritable flesh,
pursued illusion beyond the round edge
of experience and the orbiting world,
believed the wind was turned by a fist
so faceted, jeweled, encumbered with light,
mortals must be blinded by a glimpse
of one radiant knuckle. Other voyagers,

the cold still creaking in their hair,
reported an unimaginable forehead,
eyeless, Neanderthal, sloping into heaven
from the loud jaws of a gaping sea.

Some circumnavigating this circle
flee what they find, leave it for saints
or merchants to conquer, retire to rest homes,
diseases, games. Others go through
to that crevasse where the last mirror hangs
and the staring self dangles in its worn harness
over a void, while breath crashes
like a blue, falling window.

Only the mirage lives through these winters,
and the boneless wind sniffing at tracks
fixed like a wreath where the most recent traveler
has pitched his blind, enduring tent.

> *Bright southerly wind . . . low drift . . .*
> *I could see nothing . . .*
> *Bowers on my shoulders directed me . . .*
> *two long marches would land us at the Pole.*
> *. . . the only appalling possibility*
> *the sight of the Norwegian flag*
> *forestalling ours.*

Bowers' eyes were too keen,
saw almost too clearly
from his breathing roost
the unnatural shrine
at the sky's taut edge.

He felt uneasy,
tried to believe
he glimpsed only a shadow
the fumbling wind
had dropped like a cloth.

The speck seemed no larger
than the grave of a fly,
then lunged at sight,
sang like a hook,
dragged him nearer
until he envisioned
some tireless angler
turning a reel
where miles were wound
like rasping silk,
and looked through lashes
suddenly haloed
at the flag, sledge bearer,
tracks of dogs and men,
remains of a camp,
unremaining illusion.

3

It stood there pitched beyond revision,
its bamboo steeple supporting the blue,
white-bordered cross on a crimson field,
simple, deadly, compact, in order—
the other man's tent, the other king's banner,
poised at the creaking end of a journey
where orderly hope, orderly motion
become disorder for all explorers
who start too late, find the wrong weather,
misjudge the hour or the risk of arrival.

It is always too late, too huge, too little,
the island ruined, the city taken,
and we keep arriving at the place
we thought we had left safely behind us,
find the same face in the bedroom closet,
familiar dust in secret corners,

the litter staring from under the rug,
or simply the failure at the world's end
when what is attained is another journey
longer than the first and with less expectation.

The captain made his account, kept language trim,
    recorded weather, dodged despair.
Twenty-two below and a nagging chill.
    The pole was there, but no longer theirs.
His pencil bucked, paused at the edge—
    "All the day dreams must go"—
stumbled on pity. "I am very sorry
    for my loyal companions." He heard the snow,
white leaves descending over a tent
    they might never leave, felt fear
joggle his elbow. "The wind is blowing hard."
    It was nothing new. All was old here;
the trail ahead, the trail back;
    the trail back, the trail ahead,
and the future mired in the past.
    Only the chill was deeper, and dread.
Latitude eighty-nine. Drifting tracks.
    Tomorrow the wind might be a friend.
Stiff upper lip. Courage. Duty.
    Face the run home. Ascend, descend
but keep on slogging— Something whined
      and shuddered,
    invisible, huge, carrying the wind
on its own haunches, crept to his feet,
    fawned there, suffered; yet, suffering, grinned . . .
He half-nodded, dreaming, remembered too late
    It's the work that counts—could not erase
"Great God!" where his leaping pencil charged
    an indelible page ". . . this is an awful place
and terrible enough for us to have laboured to it
    without the reward of priority."

The race had been real, though the goal was false.
   He turned his back, drank English tea,
considered the eight hundred miles ahead—
   behind—nowhere—the treacherous wind,
the smoking abyss, and measured the chance
   of a green shore. It would be a near thing.

4

They stood at the mathematical point
where every direction is the same,
facing the camera's simple eye,
their own eyes blinded by a sun
that never moved, late visitors with little time
to brood on fashion or design;
still wore their sweat-stained harnesses,
shivered in baggy uniforms,
let their mittened hands droop at their sides,
furred and heavy, like severed paws.

There were no smiles, although one tried,
or seemed to try. Images blur across the miles
it takes to reach a multi-colored wheel
where drugstore paperbacks display
heroes more common to the age,
ruddier, swifter, less inclined
to risk illusion or despair.

Gray faces, gray flags. Colors were there—
though limited—the wind-charred ear,
the hidden wound growing like a jewel
on a silver heel, a blackening nail,
the violet, bone-centered chill.

They posed, exposed to the rough stare
of something beyond the winking lens—
death's head, or hope, or just our gaze

slanted across a feverish aisle
of tranquilizers, lotions, toys,
where we, like them, look past the void
to practice an imperfect smile.

III

THE JOURNEY BACK

They marched with the wind,
a south breeze behind them,
hoisted a sail
to the plunging sled,
watched it billow,
an earthly ship riding
the dreaded snow waves
of crooked sastrugi.
Runners stuck fast
where crystal showers
turned drifts to sand,
covered their tracks
as if only ghosts
were laboring onward.

It was everything now
to keep a good pace,
reach the depots
where food was cached—
Half Degree, Half Ton,
Three Degree, Summit,
Desolation, Shambles
(dead ponies waiting)—
fifty miles, ninety,
a hundred, three hundred,
thousands, a million . . .
Mathematics failed.
All miles were multiplied by hunger

and the faltering pace
of dragoon and giant,
the rusting links,
weakening members.

Wilson and Bowers are my standby.
But he stood alone, night on his forehead,
searching for error, some miscalculation.
(As a child he had been lazy,
too much the dreamer, given to tantrums,
was called "Old Moony.") He had fought back,
corrected nature. This nature was different,
and not his doing. All was risk.
That was what they had come for!
And the plan was true. No man could manage
fate or weather, or offer insurance
against chagrin. (One must preserve
a sense of proportion.)
Yet he may have missed the telling thing:
monotony, boredom, the featureless city
set beyond gardens or Monday's wash,
mailmen, the treble voice of children . . .

No, the error was failure.
Dogs might have been surer,
chops and cutlets
on the brightening snow,
but his design called for men
hauling their shadows
into a shadow. Amundsen won,
had never been moony,
knew that a whip could extend a horizon.
His mind closed, hot as a visor.

Evans' nose was frostbitten.
Oates had a cold foot.
Fifty-five miles;

four days of food.
The plan had been right,
all risks considered, but . . .
A long way to go . . .
we are pretty thin . . .
and, by Jove,
this is tremendous labour.

      The chance still held,
      in spite of blizzards
      or the sail hanging slack
      like a dirty wrinkle.
      Hope ran ahead
      with a good day's slogging.

Excellent march. Wind helping greatly.
It is all soft and sandy beneath the glaze.
Thank God, the miles are coming fast.
This is the bright side.
The reverse of the medal is serious.
Wilson has strained a tendon—
of course, he is full of pluck.
Evans has dislodged two fingernails . . .

They reached into February,
twenty-seven days from the pole,
had the summit's rock underfoot again,
felt like sailors reaching land,
stroked the dark foreheads of granite and quartz,
staggered toward knowledge,
the only prize left.
Empty stomachs could wait
while empty hands clutched
something for science.

Thirty pounds of specimen rock
was heaped on the sled that hunger must pull,

and Wilson, searching through snow-burned eyes,
found a ghost of greenery
in a black seam, memory of a leaf
throbbing on coal; imagined it growing
into branches of lilac, boxwood, laurel,
traced a numb finger along the traces
of what had been living. Blown snow rustled
like a tree, and the wind felt warmer—
while the Beardmore waited with its crevasses.

They had known the blue-gray gullets before,
vertical throats of an albino herd
buried to the eyes in basements of snow,
but direction had changed. They veered toward a trap,
teetered on chasms, found themselves blocked
by ribs of chaos, hacked a way through
but lost the day, depleted reserves,
stretched three pemmican meals to four,
prayed that the wind, and strength, would hold,
though Evans' strength had already broken.
Only a giant will, or dread, moved the giant
across the landscape. A blistered heel dragged
an extra furrow between the sledge's double track,
and Wilson and Bowers, the standbys, were blind
from the blind sun, and the effort of vision.

Breakfast tea and one gray biscuit.
The Cloudmaker ahead. Every drift held a flag
of a phantom depot. Evans cried out,
lured by a shadow. Yet a depot was there
and the speck of food that would keep them marching
toward a chimera—rain-winnowed evenings
beside a fire, a clean table sagging
with hills of mutton, veal, roast, pheasant,
jellies, puddings, buckets of gravy . . .

We have reduced food; also sleep.
A rather trying position.
Evans has nearly broken down
in brain . . .

but under the skull-surrounded mind,
the fractured will pursued a pattern:
limp on, stagger, dodge the crevasse,
remember the goal, hunt for more flags,
depots, caches, something to gnaw on,
knuckles of wind, haunch of the blizzard.
Six-foot pigmy. Fixer of sledges,
loser of nails. For lack of a nail . . .
The pattern splintered. Snow turned to a tide,
swallowed his ankles, foamed toward his thighs.

He lagged behind, swimming through marble.
They turned and waited, hauled with their voices,
made a net of smiles. He begged for a string—
excuse to linger, ruse to tie a chasm together,
lace up the void; felt the tide gather
and darkness stampede out of a cavern
that seemed within him, tore off his mittens.
The wind was on fire. He scorched his hands
in the freezing sky—tugged at his clothing—
watched his captors turn, returning,
the blind leading the blind. Only he saw clearly,
though the look was wild; and, seeing, surrendered.

He died a natural death,
and we did not leave him
until two hours after . . .

Four going on. Score One for the land.
Score Two ticking as they watched the "Soldier,"
Titus Oates, pride of the dragoons,
wade through time on swelling ankles.

Shambles Camp and a resurrection—
Snatcher, Nobby, Bones, Michael—
dead steeds that a limping rider might spur
out of congealing dust to glory,
if feet like his could reach a stirrup.

> *I wonder what is in store for us,*
> *with some little alarm*
> *for the lateness of the season.*

An old saw makes a marching rhythm.
   It is always later than you think,
And growing later, growing colder.
   A watch betrays and summers slink

Toward early winters. The final march
   Is always near, though you may think
The wind is a friend. All death arrives
   In a sudden gust, and the sun sinks

When it should rise for one more step
   Across the twilight. The brink
Seems gray beyond the miles. It is closer,
   And redder, than you think.

> *We are in a very queer street . . .*

Sunday, February 26:
   Minus seventeen. Rations short, fuel shorter.
   We want more food . . . Yet, Evans had helped a bit by
      dying.
   A march of six and one half miles at morning.
   Nine hours more; add eleven miles.
   I wish we could have some help from the wind.
   Forty-three miles to the next depot.

Monday:
    Minus thirty-seven. *Desperately cold.*
    Land disappearing in a satisfactory manner.
    We may find ourselves in safety at the next depot,
    but there is a horrid element of doubt.
    Thirty-one miles of cold remaining,
    three days' fuel, six days' food.
    Things begin to look a little better . . .

Tuesday:
    Minus forty.
    Expect we are in for a cold night.

Wednesday:
    Minus thirty-seven.
    Thirteen miles to the distance-shrouded depot.
    The oil will just about spin out . . .

Thursday:
    Minus forty-one. Cold start. Cold march.
    But the depot in sight.
    Cloudless days and nights and the wind trifling.

Friday:
    The depot reached, and doubt horribly tripled.
    Shortage of fuel, the leather-stopped mouths
    of waiting drums, wizened by cold,
    fumes sucked up by the sun's tall inhalations;
    Titus Oates' feet darkly revealed,
    the pain exposed like ten black thimbles;
    and the wind riding in on an overcast.

    In another day and month he had written,
    "The sun makes up for all evils."
    More than sun was required now,
    the season late, the wind wrong,
    and seventy miles to the next depot.

Saturday:
Amongst ourselves we are unendingly cheerful
but what each man feels in his heart,
I can only guess.

Sunday, March 4:
A white week behind them,
a white eternity ahead,
and the depot beckoning
across forty miles.
One week's food. Three to four days' fuel.
We are in a very tight place indeed.

Hope marches on mathematics—
temperature, distance, velocity of time—
tries not to perceive the oval zero
poised at the end of the wavering line.

Queer street—bad position—the wind trifling.
In a tight place, arithmetic falters
and hypotheses blow like shovels of air.
Equations snarl. One digit alters

the universe. One accidental dot—
fly speck or dust—upsets a ledger,
yet plateaus are black with men marching
toward an end they cannot measure.

These, at this pole, were decimals
set within an infinite figure;
staggered through the multiple cold
to reach the indivisible cipher.

Monday:
Regret to say, going from bad to worse.
No time for literary ornament now,

nor concern for the vanished auroral lights
that had nicked his lines with poetry
at a vanished camp. He had seen, in those skies,
ghosts leaning behind the ghostly gleams:
invisible neighbors in other worlds
sending their signals through the dark,
symbols and glowing signatures,
and had yearned for a key, thought it strange
men had not knelt and worshipped such splendor.

Now sky had become nothing but weather,
a lunatic mouth babbling of cold,
and only the wind left a signature
scribbled on snow, or set like a brand
of a white herdsman on cheek and forehead,
indecipherable, beyond translation.
The only communicant was his hand
moving by inches on a brittle page.
Some message might blaze, like those ancient lights,
across time's great and wrinkled furrow
to send, through space, its spangled cry
for men to decipher into meaning.

        Got a slant of wind yesterday afternoon.
        Converted our wretched morning run
        of three-and-a-half to something over nine.
        Started the march on tea and pemmican,
        solid with the chill off.
        We pretend to prefer it that way.
        Fuel dreadfully low;
        the poor Soldier nearly done.
        He makes no complaint,
        but he grows more silent.

All lights seemed low.

Tuesday:
We mean to see the game through
with a proper spirit.

Wednesday:
A little worse I fear.
We still talk of what we will do together at home.

Thursday:
Worse and worse in morning . . .
Oates' left foot can never last out . . .
Wilson's feet giving trouble now,
but this is mainly because
he gives so much help to the others . . .

> Thirty pounds of rock
> still rode the sledge.
> Rock of ages.
> Something for science.

Friday:
No entry.

Saturday:
Things steadily downhill.
Oates' foot worse.
He has rare pluck
and must know that he can never get through.

> Knowing is not the same as believing;
> belief is not the same as knowing.
> A little more food, a sweeter wind,
> and who knows what morning will bring?
>
> The chance may hold, the doctor says.
> But he may be lying. And God knows what
> is written down in the brown diary.

Oates is a hindrance? Oates dooms us all?
Oates must march or we cannot march?
Oates is dying? Oates is brave?

He is wonderfully brave.
He is a brave fine fellow.
Titus Oates is very near the end.
Oates is silent, knowing, enduring.
The poor Soldier has become a terrible hindrance,
though he does his utmost
and suffers much, I fear.

Suffering could end. Scott gave the order,
made Wilson unlock the crucial packet
where opium hid, thirty tabloids apiece,
with a tube of morphine left for the doctor.
Rations had always been equally shared.
No man could protest that he had been cheated—
yet death would be cheated and one's honor.

Each man drew his harness over his shoulders,
limped on, contemptuous of the bitter mercy
stored in a pocket, looked half-guilty
for the reserve filched from a deeper larder,
and carried courage like a secret
until he saw on each bruised face
the same proud guilt, the equal measure.

Oates stumbled on through four more days,
then asked to be left in his sleeping bag.
No one would leave. He must blunder on,
hauling his senseless feet beyond
horizons of sense—one step, another,
three and five, counting, falling,
lagging in time like a crippled clock;
hindrance, horror, pain's old companion.

He steered toward one more camp and slept,
prayed that he would not wake, but woke,
sloughed off his cocoon, heard the blizzard
cry like a mare, white mane blowing,
imagined silver reins in his fingers,
stood up in a shapeless uniform,
spurs missing, boots unpolished.
"I'm just going outside
and may be some time."

> They waited, knowing
> they waited for no one,
> counted each other
> in the rocking minutes.
> Three for the sledge.
> Three still marching.

> *We all hope to meet the end
> with a similar spirit,
> and assuredly the end is not far.*

Friday or Saturday:
  Lost track of dates.
  But minus forty. Minus hope.
  Number Fourteen Camp.
  Only two pony marches away
  from One Ton Depot.
  One more chance.

Sunday, March 18:
  *Ill fortune presses,
  but better may come.
  My right foot has gone,
  nearly all the toes . . .
  Amputation is the least
  I can hope for now.*
  And the most.

Would the knife hurt
if it came to cutting?
He remembered Evans,
the giant treasure,
remembered Oates,
tender with ponies,
both of them under
the white road and whitening;
saw Bowers' live eyes,
the "undefeated little sportsman,"
watched Wilson contrive
the wisp of a smile,
"the best of comrades,
staunchest of friends,"
and heard, outside,
new blizzards arriving,
clung to his pencil,
tried to remember
the day and hour
or what should be written
to those going on
in other countries:
wives, mothers, sisters,
the special friends . . .
felt the pencil stiffen.

The end was not far,
but one must reach the end,
address each letter,
reassure, comfort,
explain to the public
there had been no error,
only risks misjudged,
adventure undertaken

to the last gasp of the threshing wind;
leviathan, angel, hooked and gaffed,
the stiff wings spearing upended mountains,
flukes, white with frost, scraping a tent
of shuddering cloth, and eyes rolling.

The land itself was a whirling sky,
and the whirling sky became the land
where every definition stopped;
dragoon and doctor, pigmy, giant,
and the man who led, dissolved
and absolved in the centrifuge
that spins the world.

To Mrs. E. A. Wilson:

If this letter reaches you
Bill and I will have gone out together.
We are very near it now
and I should like you to know
how splendid he was . . .
His eyes have a comfortable blue look of hope . . .

To Mrs. Bowers:

As troubles have thickened,
his dauntless spirit ever shone brighter . . .
The ways of Providence are inscrutable,
but there must be some reason why such a young,
vigorous and promising life is taken . . .
My whole heart goes out to you in pity.

To Sir J. M. Barrie:

We are pegging out in a very comfortless spot.
I am not at all afraid of the end,
but sad to miss many a humble pleasure
which I had planned for the future
on our long marches . . .

To his wife:

Make the boy a strenuous man.
I had to force myself into being strenuous, as you know—
had always an inclination to be idle.

What lots and lots I could tell you of this journey.
How much better has it been
than lounging in too great comfort at home.

He had four days to write,
four days of blizzard
that reared between them
and the One Ton goal;
eleven miles only,
but a continuous gale
from the south, southwest.
Two cups of tea.
Two crumbs of food.

Eleven miles only,
eleven years,
time blowing in
like a sky of needles,
all things whirled
into disaster.

For my own sake
I do not regret this journey.

Perhaps they dozed,
perhaps they dreamed,
each in a sack
designed for rest
but not for a continuous slumber.
Was it Bowers or Wilson
who slept first and forever?

while Scott stayed awake
with his awful dream,
flung his hand over
the absent Wilson,
ordered his trifles—
scraps of flags,
the black flag and the other—
finished his permanent messages
to countrymen, widows,
and the admiralty.

The end is not known,
but it was never far,
as these three knew
when they pitched their house
of blowing fabric,
made it tidy
(order was a quality
apart from weathers)
made it taut,
made it secure,
the door facing down
the sharp sastrugi,
bamboos placed with a good spread,
and guarded against snow
in the inner lining.

Someone made a lamp wick
from the little fringe
of a tattered boot.
He may have written by that
or by some other wick
dipped in a spirit
jealously hoarded
against the last light.

There was surely darkness
beyond the white blizzard
and hands reaching to hands
across the crevasse
that widened, steepened,
plunged into glass,
stained windows, steeples,
churches of memory,
Christ with his lambs,
the noisy prophets,
and the world falling
but never failing
for the marchers, believers,
perdurable seekers
of the next mile, the inch,
the elaborate crystal
snow makes in falling,
eternal design of crucifix, frond,
star and odd angel.
He apologized, pitied,
put language away
and accepted the summons.

It seems a pity
but I do not think I can write more.

IV

Magellan mistook Tierra del Fuego
for the northern coast.
Drake did not like what he saw,
judged by the sample
that the hidden bulk
was not worth discovery,
looked sourly on landscapes condemned
to everlasting rigidity by Nature,
left it for resolute fools to conquer.

Merchant-adventurers sniffed the wind,
heard sirens bark from rookeries,
sailed their ships farther into shoals
where icebergs glided, large as churches
packed with gargoyles.
Islands turned red, but Weddell combined
blood with science, stuffed a seal,
gave it his name, and named a sea.
French, English, Russians, Americans
caulked their portholes against the cold,
steered toward the southern sepulchre,
recalling tales of a fertile land
hooked to the bottom of the world,
found penguins, scurvy, a million birds,
and the lucrative whale, blue as a fountain.

Some went farther, tried for the center
beyond experience or profit,
staggered back but kept on searching:
Biscoe, Balleny, Ross, Wilkes,
D'Urville, Mawson, Reynolds, Scott,
Shackleton, Amundsen, and Scott once more,
Scott forever, a part of the center,
integral, heaped there, the land's new bounty.

Its name is borrowed from the Greek,
anti (opposite) and *arktos* (bear),
that glowing mammal with the North Star
hitched to his unwavering tail.

No one knows how it began, laboring and lifting
its folded mountains, massifs, cliffs.
The sea's rough corridors were tipped
beneath some crude Pacific thrust,
and sediments soared into peaks
enclosing starfish and strange fern
whose tiny backbones sweat in rock.

Loud forests grew, when Africa was ice,
and, maybe, roses, untutored birds
with voices strained though musical.

And, it may be, trees will come again,
or glaciers turn to waterfalls
blowing like clouds, or the windy seeds
and spores of plants drift in to stamp
green hoofs upon the riderless hills,
and a skeleton wake with Lazarus eyes,
or eyes of dead explorers caught
in an iron sheath, eleven strides away
from the last cairn.
                    A leaf could crash,
yellow as thunder, or one root try
its lengthening nerve on the cloth of tombs,
pry open the tucked and pleated tents
of gathered mountains, until the whole, unlashed skull
blooms like a round and buzzing flower.

The epoch lingers and the dead stay dead,
though nothing in these latitudes can perish.
Decay is unknown, whether of flesh or language.
Hands that clasped once are forever clasped,
and love preserved is forever risen,
while the unchanging eyes, strict as jewels,
stare through a rent in the woven sky
at a sky beyond, centered on visions
we cannot cancel nor revise.

                After all, one can go on striving.
                In a brief spell of hope last night
                one heard laughter.

TWO
Captains and Tourists

ICE AGE

Often, in summer, I forget those heroes
who with white beards invaded the future
where icebergs swam like birds on water,
cold beaks turned to a ship's slaughter.

I forget, under oaks, the lack of flowers
and the tenor of dogs that must be eaten,
their bones bluer than the mouths of heroes.
But in certain dreams the fissure narrows

between cut stars and my heavy lilies
and shapes my pillow into a drift.
The future skates into my marrow.
A cap slides askew. Heroes, advise us.

DINOSAUR NATIONAL MONUMENT

By twos and threes the tourists walk
at a safe distance from the bones
drowsing beyond a balcony
designed to bridge the ticking gap
between their breath and the lost chirp,
warble, or scream of earlier lives.

Diplodocus and all his length
is nailed within the creaking rock.
Apatosaurus, hinge and spine
and scattered forehead, leans across
the leaning crowd, while workmen climb
through the dead steeples of his eyes.
Chisel and jackhammer must refine
the visible monster for our view,

peel back the mountain, expose the thighs
we could not inherit,
and the long, slow freight of vanished power.

These are no relatives of ours
and yet, from dusty holes
beneath a stunted, ignorant skull,
something looks out, returns a gaze
that seems, almost, our own—
unblinking, watchful, half-forlorn.
The quarry echoes like a vein
suddenly emptied of its blood.
A picnic basket chatters on the floor.

The other world is still,
and they are arches only, columns, groins,
pale, empty mansions fixed
in the dried flood of centuries.
Some were bird-hipped. Some had mouths
slit like a lizard's. Most loved herbs,
lilies, roots. A few ate flesh.
They were innocent, ample, doomed.
Brains small as oranges moved the weight
they had to carry. When they failed
the great tails whirred like dying clocks.

I stare into the resurrected dust,
thinking of Adam's rib and Christ's remains.
A camera clicks. Beside me,
red with sun and flesh and time,
a traveler winds a spool.
The balcony wheezes as he moves.
I watch his hips, like polished hills,
rise and descend, descend and rise,
above his deep and helpless bones.

ACHILLES

My heel always ached a little,
 as if the beak of a pin
sang there, and sometimes a nerve
 jumped like a candle. But in
those hot years when we fought
 for beauty—in ways
that made deeper wounds
 than nature gave us—the blaze
of hope seemed immortal armor.
 There were such stars then,
swimming in our shields,
 and gods blowing through men
as through locusts. Motion
 of boughs in a night wind was more
than eyes looked for; angels
 attended our wars, and the roar
of wind through our tents
 was the crimson baying of
our certain hearts. I have seen cattle
 as bright as roses, and doves
making a white ocean of a cliff
 of lilacs. But that was before
the arrow found me, small and tidy
 as a recent tooth—inquisitor,
spy—that worked like a key there,
 unfastened bad dreams,
infected the sea wind and the lost air,
 drove to extremes
the mortal desire
 to be immortal again,
until I leaped, my own arrow,
 at the perfect pain
of that wedge buried
 in the exposed cup

59

my mother missed in her prayers
    and ablution. They were not enough.
I should have gone armed
    with iron boots to my armpits,
for my heel aches now
    like a lark on a spit,
and the urn where I turn
    is a tower of myth
turned by sea scum
    and the wind's black breath.

EARLY NATURALISTS

Their eyes were sometimes weak.
Some suffered chills. Most took orders
from a priest, avoided extremes
of ape or leaf, tucked in the borders

of kitchen gardens, or fell asleep
and dreamed of plants like long-haired women;
boiled herbs with tongues and spit of eagles,
drank tea, grew old, brooded on omens,

died in their nightgowns, then ascended,
drawn toward heaven like flannel bait
past the beaks of windy hunters.
All forms, they knew, came through the gate

of narrow Eden, and all were blessed
although the sexual goat and dog
sullied the threshold. Even these, through grace,
were damp with the broad sweat of God.

A few, hot-headed, walked out of doors,
observed the manners of the shark,
the loins of roses, fever of doves,
and held a hand lens to the dark.

JOSEPH

We are never told
what the husband of a virgin,
father of a god,
did when a structure
like a black railroad sign
dropped blood at a crossing.

He may have pulled his beard
or talked with goats
white as weeds in moonlight,
or slept with his mouth open,
dreaming of girls
whose hymens he had broken
when the world was more natural.

Perhaps he squatted in that Golgotha evening,
surrounded by bats like green leather fans
opening and closing,
or the thoughts of a donkey crying
on little, hard hoofs,
inhumanely burdened
with child and mother
and a ghost like a mountain;
drew on his pipe,
smelled vinegar, a steeple
driven through his nostrils;
dozed and picked a hangnail;

snored among spears,
saw a face open
with the cry, "Father, father . . ."
and went back to his sheep
or his weeds or his sunsets,

being stepfather only,
stud, a convenience,
keeper of sperm
that rolled up the wild, wet
slope of resurrection.

REFLECTIONS OF

A GRAY FLANNEL AGNOSTIC

The world's a habit some of us never get over,
but he, I suppose, discovered ways
that led somewhere over the edge,
learned how to walk on curls of cyclones
or in the wave's slippery hammock.
His hair, down about his shoulders,
smelled of salt. More than that,
he listened often with his ear open
to what he said was a speaking heaven,
received messages from that blue mouth
which may, or may not, have been sparrows
talking more clearly than one can imagine.

He had no bad habits that anyone knows of.
It is hard to think, being what we are,
of walking past the final bar at the last hour
(the neons as bright as another year's lilacs)
before the train swerves out of the station
into the suburbs, without a quick glass,
or of never inhaling the brown breath
of one cigarette after the dinner napkin
is folded around a spilled map of gravy.

There are certain patterns scribbled on pavements
or oceans or in the clouds,
though little a common man can decipher.
Children and kittens, glossy as fire,
are frequent and distracting,
or the paper left open to a story of the Giants.

He was uncommon and therefore lonely.
Yet, he had some pleasures of a mundane kind:
the breaking of bread with rough companions,
white scent of garlic, the color of thorns
after rain fell, wood shavings, stars,
feel of a horse—donkey, rather—
lifting gray muscles between his thighs.

The worst must have been when he called the children
and saw them turn, shy and afraid,
stumbling back to their mother's aprons
to stare like flowers from that warm cover
at his breathless hair and virgin eyes.

ROBINSON CRUSOE

The sudden footprint terrified.
He felt his bones grow visible
as a white tree
and fled among the humming rocks,
exiled with his affronted mind.
The island turned to flesh,
and the raw sun
made a blue savage run with him
and with him hide.

He who had cried for company
cried for his desert soul again,
the parrot-feathered dawns,
pale goats and silences,
the guardian sea
unlanguaged and alone.

His Bible droned like a black cat;
outside, the heavy ewes complained.
The footstep thudded on a page
of Genesis and echoed there.
Perhaps the imprint was his own!
He went, and setting one bald foot
in that great spoor
felt the thin sea uprolled into an eye
and his chief terror known.

ASSEMBLY LINE

Henry had something on his mind
beyond the folderol of birds,
or horses waltzing in a field,
or loafing trees. Henry inclined
toward something practical and square,
and built it black and built it cheap
with wheels to last an average trip
(and, for emergencies, a spare).
Henry had hit on something new
to fill up dinner pails and time
and occupy men's noisy hands
and start a factory or two.

History was bunk, Henry averred
and turned a crank and set a spark,
honked at the corn and shimmied out
headlong across a neighing world;
plowed frogs and leaves and eagles under,
corrected mountains, fixed the dark,
followed a rainbow, found instead
the freeway's hot and surly thunder—
and at the end a twitching flare
like a red bush. History is junk.
Beneath, the earth is six feet deep;
the grass is optional and spare.

MODEL T

The hill was higher every year,
the old car older, less adept
at climbing up a road designed
to haul all climbers back to earth.

My grandfather pressed his muddy shoe
against the narrow, shaken floor,
and cursed the engineer who made
the world too steep. I cheered
from my safe nest behind,
where storm curtains gasped like leather birds
(in love with engines, mountains, games),
while my grandmother rocked her ridden weight
against the gravity of things,
relying on her will to aid
the long futility of iron.

We coasted down the other side
where yellow fields made a long sea.
I yearned for something tall again,
sky-scorched and wild—
then heard her wrinkled sigh
and saw his hands, grease-etched and gray,
grapple with pride
the thin and perilous wheel.

SAM'L

White hair, white suit,
a talent for truth
and putting it into words
that sounded truer,
with a wit-ring, a twang at the center.
A kitten at the ear
did not purr but "smouldered."
He hunted for this verb,
earned millions of dollars,
and pitied Lazarus
torn from his comfort;
could never remember faces
nor give up swearing;
smoked only one cigar at a time,
three hundred a month
(and a few extra)
except during courtship
when he tried abstaining
from all his sins;
desired to reform,
but managed not to,
and still won the coal-dealer's daughter,
Eve to his tear-streaked,
    profane,
        and adoring Adam.

THE STEADFAST TIN SOLDIER

Rammed into the shaft,
wedged there and sped there,
neighbor to cabbages, kleenex, letters
covered with the sorrow of ink on paper,
I tumbled through the gullet,
made friends on the way,
spoke to a cast-off tooth and trophy
and the tinsel dancer, spangled and nameless;
heard her cry, "Love me!" all the way.

We were dropped down at morning or evening
by children in shorts
and women in kimonos.
In the brown halls there were always footsteps
dragging forward or hastening away.
It made no difference what sun was rising
or what truck clattered
up what street to gather us
in slippery sheaves for a second coming
where dump fires burn into fuzzy pillars.

We went down all the way
with bones and petals
into the red ditch of the fire
especially kindled to redeem
whatever limps or leans off balance.

Only in myth does a metal heart beat
for the dancer poised on a slope of wind.
Only there does a paper boat sail
over black gutters toward a castle.
But the rat demanding a passport is known,
together with the cook—she grew up in the house,
wielding her knife, fat to her armpits—
and these ticking embers,

the tin heart cloven,
the dancer's spangle burning
like her brief and bitten face.

COMMUTER

The small skin of eyelids
shelters the traveler
through a night landscape
of wounds and wishes
where acrobats become himself
dancing on poles
or obedient stallions.
The dead mother rises,
her apron blowing
like flour in a wind.
Sleep, a long flag,
whips over meaning.
He welcomes lions
day had omitted,
climbs sexual peaks
and wrestles angels
with the eyes of an aunt
or a whiskered father.
An old sin panhandles,
dirty palm open,
or sneaks through scars
brighter than doorways.
The trip is short,
briefcase in order,
and return almost certain.
The alarm brings him up, blind,
from under his eyelids
and the dream falls
like a sock
among the spoiled linen.

PLAZA DE TOROS, IOWA

The cornhusk mattress creaks
like an empty church;
my grandfather in sleep
hunts for his death, a toreador
caught in a noise of crows and cocks.
A cat with eyes of a doll
watches from under my chair,
watching the dust that creeps.
A curtain blows like a cape.
Something whisks past,
darker than water,
louder than a leaf.

The wind is round in his porcelain mouth
where his hard breath knocks
and the bony crescents clack
like hoofs of a running horse.
The last snore comes through a canter of teeth.

The bed is still. The window shines.
Rats in the woodshed leave their chores.
The roosters cease.
A bull that panted all night long
holds his black breath
and I see his horns blue-white and cold
like the parentheses of a lyre.

ACCLIMATION

After my cousin, the choir boy,
murdered his mother with bitter candy;
and after my brother, the air force hero,
ruined his wife with a linoleum cutter;
and after my neighbor ignited his house,
and my best friend took a child to his room,
their gentle faces hung like jerky
from the live ceiling my bed looked up to.

Facts seemed fatal, at the beginning,
as the raw world must have
when it was imagined
with all its teeth and dung and passion.

Time tranquilizes, and bedrooms are cozy.
I rest most nights in the fearless moonlight
as well as the choir boy or the major
in their deep cells, or the child (grown-up now),
or the empty mothers.

Each day the pound master records the dead.
Bones of kittens burn like ignorant trees.
Headlines blur after too much reading
and the patched-up ceiling turns to mist.
I am chilled by the cold blue lisp of mice
hunting for traps arranged in my closet.
One grows accustomed even to this.

THE ALLERGIC

An angel at the door can make them sneeze
or blue light breaking from a miller's wing,
so nice is the disorder of their breath,
so windswept is the heart of everything.

Gazelles must keep in bounds, and orioles
transport their gold combines to darker trees;
the world of pelt and plume and naked rose
is battered by the dust's duplicities.

The rain brings succor, but the rain is brief;
behind it, like a horse, the black wind rears
and gallops to their nostrils. Pity these
who when they weep must weep with dusty tears.

TREASURE SEEKER

He steered into the country of success
and hung his ship upon a rock.
Hands full of seaweed, he addressed
the parrot primping in his skull:
"The land is deeper than the sea."
His parrot shone, and shouted, *Yes!*
while at his heels the ocean laid
the sunburnt hair of Icarus.

His boots, like holsters, shook the town;
he sank through gold up to his eyes,
and found five women in a bed
wanting five lovers. He was their five.
The earth around his throat grew cold.
"Women are deeper than the land."
But you are tall, his parrot wheezed.
He looked and saw. He had grown old,

with anchors hanging from his jaws
and roaring salt about his ears.
A seashell blared inside his head.
He found a blade and struck through tears
toward something flashing in his bones.
"My heart is deeper than I knew,
and full of gleams." *It can be yours*,
his prompter said. And it was true.

COMPANIONS

A leaf ran at my heels
halfway across the dusk.
It rattled like a cough.
It was as curled as an old man's
    hand around a hoe.
It was as brown as the apes.
In a gust we parted,
the leaf stumbling one way
and I another.
It was not a decision;
we merely went on separate journeys.
The wind rose behind me
and I carried it on my shoulders
    all the way
like a raving corner of the sea.

REEL ONE

It was all technicolor
from bullets to nurses.
The guns gleamed like cars
and blood was as red
as the paint on dancers.
The screen shook with fire
and my bones whistled.
It was like life, but better.

I held my girl's hand,
in the deepest parts,
and we walked home, after,
with the snow falling,
but there wasn't much blue
in the drifts or corners:
just white and more white
and the sound track so dead
you could almost imagine
the trees were talking.

EVACUATION ROUTE

Escaping the shore,
we found the mountain.
Escaping the mountain,
we found the desert.
Escaping the desert,
we found the city.
Escaping the city,
we found the sky.
Escaping the sky
we found the bee
singing inside the circular atom,

and returned to the shore
and the bones of mother, father, mistress,
children and aunts
and a hundred cousins,
and a goat whose burned eyes
resembled a brother's.
The skull of a sparrow
resembled a sister.

Escaping these bones,
we found the last fire
wrapped in the fist
of the original general.
The hard wings of his angels
were black around him
and their engines were as quiet
as the long hearts of serpents.

The fire walked toward us
with its old face shining.

It was well to be burned, then,
and escape back to the sea
where we move without hands
like red fish, through the ashes.

STAR SHOT

When the Great Bear's tail
falls like a spoon
clapping with fire,
the black wound may hold
neons for pilots
and the sailor's lost face.

I anticipate hurricanes
of white beacons falling,
which had sparks of meaning
for earlier captains,
the whole fabric tumbling
in delicate armor,
lightning unfixed,
blue spines and scales,
maps of sky upended and ended,
constellations breaking apart like forests.

Tomorrow, travelers,
behold the lacunae
of those bright towns
brought to the darkness
of this round suburb.

VACATION

Fifty dollars it cost us
for the day and the light and the weather
and a little glimpse of wind
running the waves together
over the ocean's place.
Fifty dollars and tips
for the steward who brought us ice
to cool our salted lips,
and something for the maid
who smoothed our unused bed,
and the bellboy who never caught
the sense of what we said.
We carried iron baggage,
unseasoned travelers
obsessed with destinations
beyond the place we were.
The dead moonlight pursued us
until it lost the track.
Fifty dollars and more,
it cost us to come back
out of the light and the weather
where the small wind, I suppose,
still runs the waves together
in the only way it knows.

AFTER A TOUR
OF AN OLD SAILING VESSEL

I see now why they went down
with their pianos and paintings
and sewing machines,
(a captain had one,
clever as an insect,
which sang at his prompting)

and, going down, discovered
how deep the world was,
though they had an inkling;
how they wanted brass beds
kept brighter than tigers
and decks as white as recollection
of snow falling on a favorite island;
how they watched stars open
and fondled old maps
more often than was needed;
how their kingdom was
full of swinging lamplight
(including Orion)
and leaves of canvas caught in wind,
stalks of masts blooming,
the whole, swift garden
taking them somewhere.

I see now why they went
with their roots in water
and why they swam down
to whales and fountains,
their mouths the roundest
cry of their cargos.
The ship demanded, deserved, attention
(velvets, teak, wine, and lovely breathing)
as the bottom of the sea does, being lonely.
I, too, with my insight
could drive such timbers
over the shark and sleeping oyster;
and, if the world wanted, become its diver
with a wandering cup,
going down where it matters.

NEW HARMONY

(In 1825, the British reformer, Robert Owen, tried to establish an ideal community in America, purchasing the site for his experiment from the German religious sect called the Rappites.)

1

Utopia was up for sale, plus gum trees,
vineyards, factories, hives,
and the ample blue of the Wabash flowing
past squares of barley, wheels of wind,
thirty thousand acres of Indiana,
frontier and Eden at a nominal price.

I mean to buy, said Robert Owen,
slammed his mill doors behind him like dust,
sailed from London, studied his beard,
and watched the lipless dolphins smile
across the slanted roof of waves.
Nature was instinct with happiness,
and man was answerable to man.
All that was needed was a plan
to build a terrestrial paradise
where men, not angels, could convene
around the circular throne of hope.

2

The world was water, but the ship
strode over it, bearing its burdens and his huge head
toward a purchase on a world the world would watch
in spite of snickers in the wind
from fussy lords and drowsing kings.

He squinted past the random waves
to shores invisible yet visible
within the gray hut of his skull. New Harmony.
There, other wingless, stubborn men
had charted a different paradise,
kept watch on the tall, American sky
for Christ descending toward the corn,
but found the devil, bright as a fork,
still stalking through their German barns.
They fled, leaving the sky for sale,
and the rat shining in an empty crib.

    Owen's manifesto blared in print,
    announced a new society
    far from the Old World's crimson coast
    where the chimney sweep burned with his broom
    and babies worked from star to star,
    leaving some bit of finger or thumb
    confused with fabrics of the loom;
    invited the "industrious and well disposed"
    from every land, "no references required."

3

The world was dust, but the invited marched
with kettle and flute, cradle and jug
to that green, flowing heart of land
within the core of the large brain that labeled it
"a new empire of peace and good will,"
in spite of the river's winking snags
and the serpent coiled like a hot rope
behind the searchers' searching eyes.

    Barefoot and blind, blind and shod,
    hermit and soldier, artist, thief,
    the bookkeeper racing from his desk,

the cynic fleeing toward a sudden faith,
drugged, defeated, toothless, young,
the caravan stretched like the fingers of a hand
across the passionate, April world.

Jerusalem shone among the snags.
Rocks had the look of famous towers.
Angels in aprons prepared to cook
manna from natural cabbages.

The industrious worked while the well disposed sang
under the antique light of Heaven:

Now Vice and Crime no more shall stalk
Unseen in open day,
To cross our silent, peaceful walk
Through life's enchanted way.

The tree of knowledge offered shelter,
but from its branches, some looked down
into the red mouth of the wolf, saw the ruined lamb
or the slave girl dragged like a wheelless cart
behind the fluttering hoofs of mules.
Nature was not all the dreamers had hoped.
Men were not what men had planned.

Still they came on, and the dust rose
like a rose of smoke obscuring fields
empty of farmers, forge without anvil,
churn without milk, horse without reins.

The founder dipped deeper into a valise
that carried his blueprints, clippings, charts;
corrected errors, strained toward the future
of harmony and a continuing mansion.

Society was whole, all parts related.
Negative aspects must be absorbed
in a total belief in sunrise and justice.
The whale must not suffer for the sake of corsets.
Ego must be harnessed, and circumstance altered.

The Permanent Constitution wrinkled.
Cobwebs grew like the white spines of oranges
on hoe and ridgepole, while drunkards lay
listening to a conch shell blown by a seraph:
news of good tidings and wine eternal.
Mold, a green hunchback, crept over the granary,
yet paradise endured through a second summer,
through flood and decay.
                              Some danced at twilight.
Some sat at lectures. Others crept home,
homesick for God or the cauldron of cities.

   Robert Owen proposed, his beard like a shield,
   a Declaration of Mental Independence.
   The faithful stayed on, blistered their hands,
   fought back the bobcat, scrubbed at ratholes
   as if they scrubbed a favorite jewel.
   Winter came like a plague of white locusts,
   and free minds froze deeper than metal.

Owen's faith stayed hot, though he said farewell
when the hedges whitened with a snow of flowers,
and promised new futures. Experience proved
that the next colony must be the whole world.

   He said, ". . . there is progress
   and the day is not far distant
   when New Harmony will join the ranks of the
      faithful."

He, faithful, most go, his purse filled with dust,
fugitive, wanderer in the neighing wind,
aware of the rat arranging disorder
under the lean-to of logic and science.

Disappointment was not fatal, nor graying hair.
There were other shores. Mexico waited
with its crying burros, its little servants,
and peons pushing cathedrals before them.
Mexico was a maze. Europe was another,
and man seemed in love with suffering,
seventeen-hour work days, whiskey and tyrants.
Robert Owen saw something being born,
slaved for reform, slogged over the world
with briefcase in hand, a creaking tramp,
hooted at, loved, drudge and dreamer,
beggar at the listless courts of reason.

In old age, he had a beard like a blizzard.
In age, he grew deaf, relied on spirits
lisping into his clamorous ear
of the revolt of slaves, the moral rebellion.
Small, humped, half-blind, his large head heavy
on narrow shoulders, he saw spirits perch
on the broken posts of rented beds,
traveled third class in wind-haunted trains,
planned fresh frontiers, harmonies, heavens,
tottered at last to the room he was born in
and died, believing, with his mouth open.

4

The world was smoke and his brain curled upward
into a tablet, visor of stone
where the gauze figure of Justice limps behind him,
and a caravan still marches with flute and kettle
toward Jerusalem, Moscow, Tibet, Indiana.

But the cannon blows in the whale's deep jaw.
Fabrics are flawed, still, by extraneous matter,
and nations creep toward gossamer shelters
while the sky congeals with a vibrant ash.

The world is water, yet the ship goes over,
bearing its dwarfs and generals and cargo
and his busy ghost, the knobby head turned
toward a reflection crossed by dolphins,
sharks, and missiles; seeing unions of men
united with nature; children, pinker than rolling apples,
let out to dance in smokeless meadows;
lyceums, gardens, unwalled cities . . .
New Harmony still up for option,
but the houses blind, the tenants missing.

THREE
Ants and Other Travelers

RHINOCEROS

I have never seen that beast
with his snout bearing a pagoda
and his eyes like little fragments
and his haunches carrying hills
with them. His teeth, I have read,
are monuments, and his heart colder
than a key in winter
though he sweats from pores round as goblets
full of swamps.
The white hunters have killed him
a thousand times over.

I think of myself walking toward him
and preaching a love of creatures,
leaves in my palm, or a loaf of sugar,
and his great horn still,
the knees waiting,
and between us, like birds,
a twittering hope,
or merely the pause
between monster and monster.

FROM THE LAUNCHING PAD

Oh that space monkey, soft as a hand,
that I hug, handle, dandle through other stars,
whisk through my mind, paw and pamper,
inject with solutions,
tune up with hope like an engine or gut,
aim at the moon and the leeching sun.
Will he gasp, will he purl in a dead poet's gyre?
make us new men, higher than men
at plow, pot or forge
or at the adding machine's incessant piano?
carry us out of fire to fire?

His eyes look out
like the eyes of a child becoming planets.
He leaps to farewell.
We stand by counting
on the ancestor flung over our jungles
to a sea-smear, star-wash,
whatever makes gallows of light or thunder—
until he hangs there,
brute, swinging savior
with soft hand and wound
and the sorrow of creatures.

CICADA

I lay with my heart under me,
under the white sun,
face down to fields
and a life that gleamed
under my palm like an emerald hinge.
I sheltered him where we lay alive
under the body of the sun.
Trees there dropped their shadows
like black fruit,
and the thin-necked sparrows came
crying through the light.

At my life line I felt
his bent, bright knee
work like a latch.
He was safe with me
in the room my round bones made—
or might have been—
but he sang like a driven nail
and his skinless eyes looked out,
wanting himself as he was.

Wisdom was imprecise,
my hand's loose judgement dark.
Some jewel work straining in his thigh
broke like a kingdom.
I let him go,
a jackstraw limping to the dynamo
of hunger under the hungering sun
and the world's quick gizzard.
High noon hummed,
all parts in place—
or nearly so.

MOTE

The hummingbird, acquaintance,
hanging at the feeder,
fencing with his beak,
suspended as by whirling arms
or two round harps,
is instant color.

Here we have a minute thunder,
mandolin, banjo, fever,
potential crisis of motion
as in a spinning jenny
grown eccentric, its cotton raveling
into a knot like a flower.

This spinner ends in rainbow,
and so begins.
(The inside of the egg, surely,
is a centrifuge of opals.)

He rests, rarely and neatly,
after his spike explores
honey trapped in glass and jasmine.
He goes to that rest so swiftly
he is nearly a myth. He becomes
a bud on a twig of a bough.
He dives into wind as into water.
He lifts himself, or is lifted,
into a feathered diamond
greener than the leaves
he brings his light to.

He is an uncertain visitor,
unpredictable, fickle, late to appointments,
obsessed with nectar in distant cabinets.

But when he comes, shining the window,
and leans there, gleams in his cape,
tips his javelin and remains,
we lay down our books, music, cards,
and watch like the cats
who are also our boarders,
as helpless as they
to stay that mote by talons or love.

JACK RABBIT

The borrowed light went through the dark
where a beast with petals on his head
sent the light back from one wild eye
and turned his haunches into stone.
My hill is high; the ditch pretends
to shelter wanderers like these,
but there's a curve where power counts

against fluff scrambling onto roads
we built to carry our own lives
between black trees and staring weed.
He huddled into fear and stayed.
Below, a town of ignorant frogs
squatting in some unrented pond
stroked like one green and noisy heart.

One of us would have to wait,
or gamble for the right-of-way.
I had seen the losers stretched
along the highway's stinging belt,
small carpets laid out suddenly
beneath an unequivocal tire.

He kept within his stapled bones
and still his eye looked out and gleamed.
My brakes were never meant to hold
on such a slant for such as he
caught in a habit of response

too old to change. And yet I stopped.
And yet I spoke
until he turned and easily took
his tail and ears up the same road.
My car, a thundering shepherd, coaxed
him over the hill, and I went on.

AFFINITIES

Dusk is in the cat.
It stores its shadow
in the black loft of his bones
where his ribs hang
from the spine rod.

Thunder's loose guitar
is in him,
in miniature,
and the thistle's fire.
The world is sharper
for the shape of his ears
and the blue wishbones of sparrows.

AQUARIUM

The sea, blue grinder,
    sampler of cities and horses,
    collector of engines,
touches more simply the whale,
    he of the bulged forehead
    and watery vision;
making room for his spout,
his moving anchors,
his hauled belly scraping an island
    or a hidden sailor
        so that he in his blue habit turns,
        eyes shut like the skin of a gull.

THE BEAR WHO CAME TO DINNER

Where he rows the dark
any door will do.
You can't keep him out;
he'll cellar through
keyhole or crack
on his bearded knees
if yellow once twangs
in your black like bees.
You can't keep him out,
yet you can't have him in
like a cave in the house,
haunches and chin
dripping cold bees
on a Queen Anne chair,
moss to his ears
and mildew for hair.
He'll thumb back your lids
in sleep for a lark,
breed moths in your bed,
and snore like a harp.
There's nothing he won't,
and nothing he will,
but he'll lug the whole dark
across your door sill.

BEEF TONGUE

This sang F-sharp once;
even eyes spoke
when the knife winked
and ran at its work.
The abattoir is a vocal place.
But cold as the sea now, on my plate,

(and like a branch from the sea,
pink-furred and mossed,
buds brushed in rows
where hunger washed
hayfields one way
to the garrulous rooms
of stomach or gut)
it lies, dark red,
absurdly huge
for the little it said.

INVASION

The city stopped,
confounded by bees
stewing like a kettle
in a trusted tree;
slanting and shining
in yellow suspense
above the sidewalk's
common sense.
Patrolmen, alert,
fled to their cars
to brood on honey
escaped from jars,
while hucksters and dons
departed from
the simple tree's
delirium.
Something too primitive
and plural
had balked at being
strictly rural.

Nothing is safe
if kettles of bees
can thunder and shine
in city trees.

KINGFISHER

Light was blue
with the color of this bird
going through it;
and he, between his wings easily,
turned bluer where water was,
where fish were in water,
where blue coming through blue
became something other,
became light in circles
without stopping
until one circle was,
abruptly,
his wide, white eye.

THE NEIGHBOR

From a cave of bricks I called the racoon;
plunging through tires I sang to the locust;
against all traffic I prayed for a fawn;
beyond the suburbs I sought a country;
found a wild acre and planted my will there;
discovered new chaos, old boots, dead chairs;
hammered my thumbs, impaired an ankle—
but called the racoon, remembered the singers,
pictured deer moving like branches of felt
down to that hill. Morning had lions

of fog to build. Green stars constructed
an infinite bear. One bony mouse coughed
in my cupboard. I staggered hope fast
to wildness and stayed there,
called to the fox, invited the badger,
yearned for a tiger, a cub, an eagle;
once heard a lizard scratching an answer—
and then, at dawn, the easy footsteps
of something moving into my landscape.
A cold sun lighted a mongrel face.
The eyes were love-haunted; the yellow tail
wagged the brute hill aside, and tamed it.

SONG OF THE FLIES

Praise to the god of fish
    who out of the lake's blue thighs
delivers such largess:
    dead silver and dead eyes.
The evening beaches shine
    with ruin, like sleeping armor,
and bounty leans in drifts
    where our black nations murmur.
Blessed be hook and hand
    and the cold sigh of the net
and the fisherman's round back
    bearing its cape of sweat.
Praise, too, for newest hawks
    and the plunging light that pries
open the tuna's breast
    where the sea explodes, and skies
of sailors fall and drift
    with puckered mouths toward treasure
already heaped in coves
    by a hand too tall to measure.

TOAD

This shiny prince infects, they say,
the curious thumb.
Warts grow like cities
until some hands reflect
pale bumps of jewels
as if his kingdom, after all,
had power to afflict
what cannot love.
I, commoner, have seen
his chinless profile turned
to princesses in guise of gnats
or queens laced in obsidian
like precious flies—
until the fisherman's deep palm,
immune to myth,
surrounds his furious skin.

WARNING

It was heaven-hot here, a heaven-held day,
though Pacific-cold where the combers
    descanted
west of the Golden Gate, and rockward,
pluming brown shoulder and cheek and ankle,
and he plowed to the blue, beneath the ocean,
where the gray, unspotted and lean knife lay
with teeth like a forest. He had no warning
before his arm screamed, the sudden bone
    finding
a mouth as vocal as a saw in winter,
while his other mouth cried, "God! Shark!"
    together,
as if both were the same and both out hunting,
wrapped in the same wet shadow.

His girl tread the spongy world beside him,
a spindle of breath, half-naked dreamer
waking to that broth of an unknown sea
where roses tumbled, rambled and rotted
and the thorn of bone which skin had clothed
on its special trellis, white as a monster;
yet swam to his wounds, searching a finger,
hair, head, shoulder, whatever could be lifted
nearer the warm sky—though sea was warm now—
and a sickle-mouth hungered. He was slash and
    sorrow
and she rowed him like ribbons, raveling deeply,
to the shore he missed by his careless dying.

Tourists and seekers, remember the experts
who told us the deep had no interest in divers;
think how our ocean promised coolness
and how the hot shark boils in harness
though he comes like a shadow through shadow.

LOVERS

They each came armed with favorite stones
and each an awl, and each a blade,
and both wore mouths as delicate
as the pink, closing gills of fish;
kissed, mauled, despaired, caressed and struck
and wondered that their modern hearts
concealed such racks of ancient tools.

I need, I want, I fear, they cried
above the slamming doors of breath,
and ran down corridors as dark
as the insides of guns or flowers,
while hate knocked like a wandering bone.

Outside, their two soft spaniels sat,
pawing the noisy door for love.

ANTS AND OTHERS

Their spare, fanatic sentry comes
across the miles of afternoon
and finds us out, our single crumb
left dozing in a yellowed spoon;
sets up his wireless, reports
to Brown Shirts, comrades, pantry thieves.
(Their army goes like coffee grounds
down doorknobs, drains, up balconies
we meant to guard from minor lusts,
but lacked the key or missed the time.)
Defenseless now the last crust leans
beside a cup. The brown knots climb,
as neat as clocks. I feel the heat
of other lives, and hungers bent
on honeycombs that are not there,
and do not ask what sweet is meant
for which of us, there being such need
of loaves and fishes everywhere.

FOUR
Survivor: West Coast

MIRAGES

*. . . the surviving horse, driven frantic by thirst, thrust his mouth
into the flames of a campfire under the illusion that it was water.*

World of the Desert—Ernest

Pegasus found shelter in the heavenly stalls of Olympus . . .

Mythology—Hamilton

. . . How the sand came at us, color of Corinth
and broken cornstalks,
how the wind burst its bag of clouds,
how we sought an oasis as green as Iowa,
how the camels stank and at night chewed their cuds,
how by day their legs rowed like leather oars
through the hot, blowing sea,
and their eyes shone as through brown water
while the impatient horses (brittle possessions
the nomads say, but good for war)
were forever hungry, thirsty, or dancing,
whinnying around the coffee fires
and the tents pitched like motionless waves.

. . . How I groomed one horse (one I brought with me
out of harness and the shadow of silos,
though he had drunk at the hippocrene spring),
rubbed him as bright as a birch in sleet . . .
how I fed him herbs so crisp they chirped
between his teeth, and the milk of camels,
bringing it in bowls, the warm foam frothing
whiter than his blizzard-thick, sun-scalded mane . . .
then escaped the herdsmen with shrewd rat faces,
and the women working at their shrill distaffs
(none was an explorer, none sought the horizon
with its blue harbors, chimeras, temples),
galloped off like a sail under billowing starlight.

. . . How we saw before us, just before dawn,
the five-fingered hand of the desert hare,
and thought, for an instant, we were saluted.

. . . How the sun thickened and the wind changed;
heat was a gong in a brass bell's throat,
lamenting, loud; how we passed the hedgehog,
the wolf, and vermin, and seed-hunting ants
heaped over with cargo; how the scorpion
lifted his pallid steeple; how the carrion eagle,
small but sudden, turned as we turned;
how the sun fell in ruins at every sunset,
and frost rose like needles;
how we licked the cold dew
and shivered together, heart to haunch,
yet dreading the furnace of the sun's resurrection—
and sought Olympus beyond the next morning.

. . . How we descended craters, ascended sandstone,
lost the compass in a drifting castle,
tripped on thorn trees and went on, pawing bronze spaces—
I in my armor, he in his bridle—
and how, near the end, I had to tug him,
how his white mane thawed,
how when we found water
(bones in it and shrapnel)
it crackled like fire
between his dry teeth . . .
how we were troubled with gnats and leeches—
dark wreaths for his eyes—
and how sky and sand became lava.

. . . How I searched for searchers, and how I listened
for a camel's cough or the whine of a distaff,
and yearned in my throat for dark rain or wine
or the locusts roasted for a stranger,
but fought back a surrender to these gods.

. . . How it was my steed who ended the journey
and threw me, returned to a plow horse,
acquired visions of commonest clover,
brayed with thirst like a saw, forgot his wings,
sought for a pond in a plain farmer's pasture,
grew a wild eye that rolled like a marble.

. . . How when I kindled an evening fire
he mistook the flames for water,
plunged his mouth in and gulped the red fountain,
screamed like a wire, and leaped upward,
his nostrils streaming gray roses of smoke . . .
                        how I went, blinded, back
to the hair-cloth tents, the herdsmen and housewives,
the sound of the coffee pestle, the snores of old men,
the wells stained yellow from pollutions,
my beggar's bowl always extended.
. . . How I, like Bellerophon before me,
grope through the stalls of dust,
unmoved by hope or hoof or caravan
beneath the nickering sky.

BROBDINGNAG

The owls roost like gray lamps up there
above the firebreak and weeds
where we never venture after dark,
wicks of ears blowing in a fir-black wind,
eyes (rounder and simpler than our own)
staring down at this estate
toward the picture window we cannot close
to any viewer, wise bird or beast.

We bought for privacy here,
but shadows become, in the electric glare
of anniversaries or games,
improbable animals on a visible wall:
giraffes on hassocks or in easy chairs,
fauns shuffling cards, blue apes and swans
waltzing across the rumpus room
until they splash from the ceiling and fall
like mammoth commas in a bed.

Even after hours, shadows may sprawl,
larger than life, on a drunken field.
I have no fear for these, but fear
when the wind is high, and bats are few,
how some sad, dwindling shape of ours
could creep through silver husks of fog
and seem to those above, a smaller thing
than we conceive ourselves to be:
more mouse than giant, more creature than man
and vulnerable to watching beaks.

Still though they are, with talons shut
around a waving branch,
they could drift down.
I have wakened often from a cold dream
and smelled the smoke beneath their wings
and seen their eyes this side of the pane,
hot and intent with a strange love
for what they can light upon and keep.

ARM CHAIR TRAVELER

My senses are green with a dream of fruit,
birds blue-black as storm in the Dakotas,
and the stale odor of rain
combed through a pride of lions.
The moon leaps over Minnesota
like a white-faced clown
and I hear palms speak to each other,
rusty as yesterday.
The sea of salted Asia
walks on my eyes.
I live in a box in California
under the wild, unwarranted sun
and the wind pulls my hair like a parrot
whose head blossoms with rubies.

It may be I shall find an island
in Tibet or Spain or Kansas
or the spoiling blue of Oahu
for my senses are dark with roots
and the wire laughter of monkeys.

ALBUM PIECE

I thought then, on that lake
where our rowboat went
with a lantern in its beak,
I will take this event
and these faces from the dark
to a sill reserved
on a future alley
where what is preserved
will warm my future:

Spears of pike turned
under white-necked oars
and I kept what I learned
from Wisconsin water.

A whole carp rose
through hooks of starlight;
dark held its pose
against speculation,
and the long pickerel hid.

I said I would save
what I could, and did.

CLAIRVOYANCE

This is my time of attention
to the angels in sparrows and boxes,
and the light in animals.
I have a ghost in my hand.
Touching rock or forests
or the brass of a lion,
I have met surprises richer than sunsets.

This hank of wood,
skeined like the leg of a deer,
misses some part of itself:
a hoof like a fingernail,
and the haunch, brown, in its holster.

DEAR SIRS

I apologize for the crayon scrawls
on my income tax statement,
and regret that kitten tracks mar
my last mortgage payment,
or that my hand trembled in signing a protest
against the most recent, special assessment.

I ask indulgence in the matter
of scattering my cocker's ashes
from an urn neither authorized nor rented
by the society of morticians,
or for watching a wren poised on a billboard
without reading the earnest message.

I admit to walking sometimes at evening
on freeways the deer and the woodchuck created,
and of sitting in a hammock while commuters surge
homeward to gin and the dusk's occupations.

I have been ignorant of certain laws
but beg exemption for the time being,
being pledged to prior commitments.
The canary has the croup. The baby is feverish.
Our cat has delivered a blind litter.
Weeds are consuming my stock and roses.
There is a new crack in the foundation.
Winter is approaching. The wind sounds hungry.

LABORS

The ceiling was hot under the cold sky
while the forceps probed; the creature that
   was I,
wrapped in my cave, fought back the light
falling like steel and the blizzard-bright
blood drifting over fists and eyes.
                  My mother rocked
like the storm in the stove, and my heart knocked
at her latched bones, and my father ran down
                the single street
of so sad a town that only winds meet
in its frequent alleys.
                   The doctor's tools
must have been clean, or else only fools
survive a labor of the kind we put in—
she alive (and I just barely) and the din
of breath beating louder than the pipe
of the raw, black stove where the ripe
wood was born again through fire.
                 In the rack
of other nights, I feel myself falling
                through the stack
of that blind flue and its crying wood;
gill-free and toothless, the enormous hood
of a former darkness pulled down over the scar
I have almost conquered.
                 Where we are
now is no stranger than where we have been
or where we are going. I seem to hear the thin,
barbaric cry one of us gave—or it may have been
   only the doctor's sigh
as he limped home, chilled, under the steaming sky.

GHOST

Dream is a darkness troubled by sisters,
mothers, a friend, the wraith of a fish
with a hook in both eyes, a pet dog dying
and resurrected like a Christ in fur,
and black umbrellas that refuse to open.

Last night I saw her, helped her to the table,
lied about pain, forced her to eat
out of my hunger. Tablespoons lay crooked
against the oilcloth, and my hand was an animal
trying to correct them.
"We'll put them straight tomorrow," I said,
but told another, "She'll be dead by then."
As she was, and is, with the spoons still crooked.

I believe in ghosts.
I lay awake, dreaming, looking at grass
in the living moonlight—and something chirred:
frog, cricket, bird. For a moment I thought
it was a voice that mattered.

PERSONAL GEOLOGY

Hurdling as a rock over wind,
I perceived gravity and came down,
making a loud hole in the foundation.

I have a corner of the basement to myself
and have become a proper boulder,
quiet, wearing a little moss on my forehead.

The wrinkles of my thought are sometimes mistaken
for a past under oceans
or in the red gizzard of a volcano.

Stones may know more than you do
and have longer legs.

MEMORANDUM

In the history of evenings,
footnote the locust
with his dry lip mourning
the haystack's summer,
and the beetle driving her paper coach
over a lamplit fever of ditches.
Make note of crickets
like straw men hanging
out of the broken hair of meadows,
boots to their thighs,
with clocks laced under;
and how at the leaving sky
bats flung their leather shadows.

Remember wagons of stars
pausing beyond the street light,
the Great Bear tacked in his harness,
and over the wooden village
the last, brown stitch of a swallow.

Put down a lamp's tulip of flame
and the moth's cold fist at my window.

THE FINAL BARN DANCE

The dark, rural cry of heifers
surprised the dancers a little,
and the clack of green parasols
where rooted clover moved
in a wind older than barns
and nearly as old as money.

Hills which had just been sold
to developers of the country
leaned on a siding of sky
over new lambs and a sow
displaying a valentine rump
behind the deodorized door
specifically labeled WOMEN.
MEN had a different arrow.
The world was segregated
beyond the power of love,
and clouds had moved in early.

We sat with other strangers
chewing the blood of steers
that a few, sage cooks had murdered.
I glimpsed the ranch's last owner
in the loud light of the bar,
a flute of grass in his teeth.
His denim body was posed,
as slim and committed as money.

NATIVE LAND

In that country the wind
in his howl jackhammers
hawks from their wheels,
and ice boards up the pickerel's
    comet
and staples the carp into his meadow,
and the runners of sleet
through the metal forest
buckle the rabbit's eye to his
    eyelid.
In that country a wolf
with a tin face follows
the grooves of a doe,
her knees unfastened,
and a mouse staggers
under the cliff
of the raven's boiling shadow.

PENTHOUSE INDIAN

My concrete tipi
lacks the round lake
and the pines humming like spinsters.
Cars come in the evening,
swifter than hummingbirds,
and twilight rattles
like a tin animal.
In the night dogs holler.
The badger is silent,
and the moss-headed buffalo.
The mouse tries his claw
on my cement clothing.

In darkness I see the spark
of his endeavor.
I shall get up at morning
and sharpen my arrows,
shooting them at glass
and insurance buildings.

PROBLEMS OF TECHNIQUE

I wish to imitate the blue of certain evenings
by look or gesture
or by an invention like the wind
which uses the speech of towers
and the running hair of women.
Blue is difficult—
as witness, sometimes, water,
or the sky going down
red as a target.

REAL ESTATE

The concept of paradise
is of something which can be lost
as most gardens are lost
to the snail and the earwig.
Renters and squatters have multiplied
in my western back yard
and trash piles up on the patio
we retired to in hope of angels.

Exhaust and exhaustion plug the sea;
the jellyfish sprawls with its lavender engine;
the dead whale rots near picnic grounds;
oranges, elected kings of color,
die for the bulldozer whose cold snout goes
clothed in forests and other flowers.
Walnut trees with their brain-shaped kernels
buckle and break from disease and tractors.
The hummingbird falls in cement and becomes
a hot and tiny, whirring statue.
Real estate is real for those believers
in brick, steel, stone, and life-proof stucco,
who trade on a future untroubled by gardens
or the warp of great trees speaking to clouds
as they spoke, I presume, to an earlier landlord
who borrowed one leaf to keep from going naked.

GOOD SUNDAY

How sleepy I become when I look at my life
as on a Sunday when there are no parties
or other events of consequence
except the trip to the laundromat,
pulling a cart behind,
or catching up on war and peace;
the jungle idleness of leaves
and sunlight falling
makes one think of sleep and death
and sleep again,
and Monday rolling onward like a stone.

I have seen my face hung in the frame
suspended from a bathroom wall
where all of us see ourselves and wink.

I have imagined behind these blood-laced eyes
the personal skull,
the noisy heart which thuds
above the whispered truth or shouted lie,
and the determined hair sprouting
in spite of gravestones overhead
or the mower's green, revolving teeth.

I lean and look
through half-shut lids
on weekends which I meant to save
by hope, communion, clean socks, or love.

Flesh closes all eyes. I stretch and snore,
protected from most incidents
though the crash of leaves comes through,
it being the time of fall and rot.
A neighbor's distant radio
yaps of a foreign woman who flees
a hut on fire. (The soldiers watch.
Rice and wood have to be burned
for the enemy must neither eat nor rest.)
She runs through my dreams
and the drifting sun, dragging a cart,
her child like a naked doll in her arms,
barefooted, bent,
all the bones of her face awake.

Heat lightning shivers like a drum
above a neon-lighted bar,
while thunder hauls
its long, slow wagon over iron.
My newspaper rattles at my feet.

The Sunday afternoon is pricked with storm,
but safe. I fold the stock reports with care
against my eyes, and sleep.

RHYMING DICTIONARY

Cat gut is clear-cut
but the halibut's shine
has a super-fine edge
like a sledge runner lashed
to blue, thrashed snow.
Shades I know can excite
by a light less clear
than a bright spear gleaning
the meaning of a stream
or the seam of a shark
making dark come
with a hum of blood.
Even the mud of things
can become springs
of frightening lightning
and bloom white with doom
clear-cut as cat gut
in a hut where thumbs
strum what is hung
over the halibut's
cut, red head.

STORMY RECEPTION

The lightning's broken fences fall
against the wires of the wind
and crackle where De Forest found
a way to trap the verbal skies.
Blue glimpses came into his mind
(though space barked like a rabid wolf),
the volume low, the treble high.
He boxed them neatly on a shelf
with room for angels, cooks, and spies.

The evening light is swift and sly,
embellishing the polished cage,
but sound is fickle, troubled by
the sudden burning of a wave
an inch away from hearth and home.
We listen to ourselves alone.

Above the crooner's blue lament,
preceding songs and psalms to cars,
the fruit that our first mother prized
swings like a bird upon the wind
and falls, tooth-marked and shrill,
across our silent, silent lives.

SUSPENSE

The whirlwind has not walked
over this country lately,
nor the corn taken up arms against us.
Birds flash in their scarves, still,
and the snails leave white embroidery
on the sidewalks at morning.
There are signs of change
where the wet horizon burns like a dancer
and fish glow suddenly,
soft bellies upward.
Grass has not learned it yet,
nor the orange light flickering
in a tiger lily.

OCEAN

It is all mountains running away in one direction.
It is an amphitheatre of gray, wet locusts.
It is a ranch of colts.
It is a great mouth of pebbles arguing together.
It is the socket of whales and algae.
It is a pasture of wind; it is a trough
   uplifting pink rinds and rubber.
It fills up men's mouths.
It washes the rounded skulls of sailors.
It nourishes the gull and the single-minded shark.
It rejects the owl and his boat of feathers.
It is full of salt.

   I am not its tenant but a neighbor only,
   using it on weekends for a glimpse of horizons
   or just the rough edge that seals look over,
   connoisseur of its drifting serpents
   and wooden angels, collector of sand
   for cats and children, beachcomber, thief,
   my pockets creaking with the abandoned castles
   of star and urchin, a spy observing other travellers
   who haunt the edge, each supporting his pail and shadow,
   sun lotion, hamper, private expectation
   at the land's end or the land's beginning.

Sometimes, at midnight, far from all neighbors,
caught at a corner, waiting for a signal,
I think of starfish lost in cupboards,
sea shells humming in dusty closets—
or an angel sprawled in weeds by a driveway,
the awkward host we could not carry
into apartments already cluttered,
salt piling up, invisible,
from under our small and mourning eyelids.

SURVIVOR: WEST COAST

Rain here has long eyes
and the wind smells like peeled
  apples
coming in on a sea
in the shape of little soft
  boats without sails.

The last tide,
full of islands,
covered half a city
and left many bones
for the rain to look at.

Searching through salt
and the hot rain still falling
  like trees
I remember the smiles of generals
  and acrobats
and the color of the sky
  in their mouths.

YOU ARE INVITED

The recorder squats in an alcove
preserving the cries and disorder
of our most usual party,
the cough that follows our wit,
the hiccup demeaning sorrow.
From spools in a special cupboard,
safe from small teeth and error,
we play back yesterday's rituals
when we were different persons,
the long bracelet unwinding
and time's wrist short and naked.

We listen to other selves
at a picnic or a dance or a war,
reciting old jokes and opinions
grown older through resurrection,
and a ghost extends an elbow
against a rib, and startles.
Uneasy, we smile at the strangers
we have become, interlopers,
memories off key, years garbled,
noisy above the bottles
pouring tomorrow's potion.

Grass is usually quiet.
Snails as noiseless as water
go over the painted patio
where a sandal scuffs like-a-word.
A lighter clicks above traffic.
Past the edge of our hearing, trains
stamp their black hoofs on tracks
that neither save nor remember.

Our voices unwind forever
for the sake of a future audition,
our host's or our own or a stranger's.
Silence, if it happens, is awkward
and someone must counter quickly.
By mistake, once, thunder spoke
and the head of a lion rolled
between us and our laughter.

PRIVATE SHELTER

The bed beneath the ground is frilled
with chintz as blue as the lost sky,
and every week the neighbors lead
their dancing children to the room
decaled with Mother Goose and stars,
under the rosemary and the roses.

One must practice to survive,
and listen for the trumpet blast,
watch sun and leaf, translate all omens—
a kitten's cry could be the sign,
the wilted faces of cabbages
bought at the safeway, guaranteed fresh,
or the sudden, inexplicable stain
on the lip of the friendly dog next door.

Threat can be subtle; death can be slow.
The burrow is deep, equipped with toys,
canned goods, bandages, a deck of cards;
too much leisure can corrupt
whether above or under the ground.

Hell, not angels, waits overhead
and salvation is for the provident
robed in concrete. They may see,
wading through bones of robins and cities,
what I hope I shall never see,
watching here from my paper tent
the elaborate roof and pitch of stars
slung over a ridge that seems everlasting.
My shelter is what I know and love:
this grass, these friends, this enterprise
of earth and air, and the ignorant owl
singing as if all owls were immortal.

I fear for the prudent, breathing like moles,
and survivors crawling into a world
where nothing moves but their crawling shadows.
I am concerned for wives and mothers
tumbling toward graves they must keep cozy,
and fathers with slide rules, working late,
promising ramblers and resurrection
out of flame and their own seedless ashes.